THE WIFE OF HERACLES

Uniform with this volume

EURIPIDES

ALCESTIS (*24th Thousand*)
BACCHAE (*31st Thousand*)
ELECTRA (*50th Thousand*)
HIPPOLYTUS (*38th Thousand*)
IPHIGENIA IN TAURIS
(*32nd Thousand*)
MEDEA (*33rd Thousand*)
RHESUS (*9th Thousand*)
THE TROJAN WOMEN
(*39th Thousand*)

ARISTOPHANES

THE FROGS (*24th Thousand*)

SOPHOCLES

OEDIPUS, KING OF THEBES
(*24th Thousand*)
THE ANTIGONE (*4th Thousand*)

AESCHYLUS

AGAMEMNON (*12th Thousand*)
THE CHOËPHOROE (*5th Thousand*)
THE EUMENIDES (*4th Thousand*)
THE SUPPLIANT WOMEN (SUPPLICES)
(*4th Thousand*)
PROMETHEUS BOUND
(*4th Thousand*)
THE SEVEN AGAINST THEBES
(*3rd Thousand*)
THE PERSIANS (*4th Thousand*)

THE ORESTEIA
(collected edition)

THE WIFE OF HERACLES
being Sophocles' Play
THE TRACHINIAN WOMEN

Translated into English Verse

with explanatory notes

by

GILBERT MURRAY
O.M.

*Formerly Regius Professor of Greek
in the
University of Oxford*

LONDON
GEORGE ALLEN & UNWIN LTD

FIRST PUBLISHED IN 1947

PRINTED IN GREAT BRITAIN
in 11-*Point Caslon Old Face*
BY UNWIN BROTHERS LIMITED
WOKING

PREFACE

THE *Trachiniae*, or *Women of Trachis*, is one of the plays which takes its name from the chorus, like the *Trojan Women* or the *Suppliant Women*. But whereas those names give some idea of the subject of the play, the title *Women of Trachis* suggests nothing. For that reason among others I have adopted in this translation a different title, "The Wife of Heracles."

It is in many ways a difficult play, though a very fine one. All critics speak with admiration both of the dramatic poignancy of its central scenes and the singular beauty and delicacy of its character drawing. Yet it has caused in most of them a sort of bewilderment or dissatisfaction, a feeling that there is something wrong somewhere. The cause of this dissatisfaction is without doubt the character of the hero. Heracles is one of the most fluid and variable of all great figures of Greek legendary tradition, but nowhere is he quite as unsympathetic as in the *Trachiniae*. This observation is not a new twentieth-century eccentricity. Some 150 years ago, Hermann explained that, while the poet's real subject was obviously the death of Heracles, he had by inadvertence made Deianira much more interesting than his hero, and thus confused his drama. Even before Hermann, Jacobs had argued that the true theme of the play was the disastrous influence of Erôs, as illustrated by its effect on Heracles. Jebb on the whole agrees with Hermann. He describes the

5

action of Heracles as "brutal" and "inhuman," and at one cardinal moment regrets that Sophocles "misses an opportunity of removing a great impediment to sympathy." Professor Webster similarly in his chapter on Character Contrasts makes Heracles the champion of "prejudice" and "faithlessness."

Was Sophocles so inexperienced or so unskilful a dramatist as to make his hero "brutal," "faithless," and comparatively uninteresting, by mere inadvertence or the missing of dramatic opportunities? I cannot believe it. If he had meant to make his Heracles a typically heroic or sympathetic character, I am fairly sure he could have done so. If he has presented Heracles in this repellent light he did so intentionally and had good dramatic reasons for doing so. Let us read the play straightforwardly and see what its actual effect is.

We hear of Heracles first as he appears in Deianira's eyes. He is her deliverer from a still more awful suitor, and she adores him. He is "the best of men," the "ever-victorious." If he is always away from home and hardly knows his own children, if he treacherously murders an unsuspecting guest and thus forces her and her family into exile, she never thinks of criticizing him. Next we have the news of his conquest of Oechalia, his triumphant return, and a general paean of joy at his victory interrupted by the entrance of a terrible procession of captive women, who are kept before our eyes, suffering and speechless, through the whole of a long scene. Deianira at the sight of them is so swept by "an awful pity" that her congratulations fail her and turn into fears. She speaks especially to one noticeable young captive, who is really the princess Iolê, but gets no answer. The girl has never spoken nor ceased weeping since she left her city, "swept through by the wind." What has caused this misery? We have Lichas' account of Heracles' murderous grudge against Eurytus, and his outrageous revenge against Eurytus' city. It is a bad story, but even so it is not the truth. The real motive for this wholesale slaughter, we discover, was not revenge, a comparatively respectable fault in a hero, but a demand from one "who has had more women than any living man," (l. 460) to have the princess as his secret concubine. These enormities might perhaps be forgiven if, when Heracles himself made his appearance, he showed any sign of magnanimity or pity. But no, there is not one. Only terrible outcries of pain, curses on his bearers, curses on Deianira, curses on Hyllus, partially redeemed no doubt, as must be expected, by unshaken courage towards death.

Against this terrific being stands the lovely figure of Deianira, the most tender and beautiful, and perhaps the most delicately studied, of all the female characters in Sophocles. The love of man has come to her only in the form of a savage possessiveness; her own love is a devotion which neither cruelty nor unfaithfulness can shake. She is herself, as her name perhaps implies, a prize of battle carried off by the victor, "like a lamb torn from its mother" (529 f.). No wonder from girlhood onward she has been haunted by fears, first a fear of love itself; later on, fears on behalf of husband and child. She is no fool. She knows men's weaknesses; she knows the world and can face its disappointments; her one clear ambition is to be a blameless wife to "the noblest of men." At the height of her disastrous failure she is comforted by the thought that Hyllus, at least, (748) had found his father and stood by him to the last. For her own error she has no word of excuse or pleading. She takes a sword and dies like a soldier. There is great drama here, and drama dependent on the brutal hardness and selfishness of Heracles. Deianira is a type of that utter devotion sometimes shown by women to the domineering force of the fighting male. One may think of Barrie's "magerful man," of the Brontë heroes Heathcliff and Rochester; even of Robert the Devil or of Bill Sykes, or of the old proverb about a peculiarity said to be shared by women with dogs and walnut trees. In most of such studies the "magerful man" is made to show some unexpected tenderness or magnanimity which idealizes him, or at least swings the sympathy suddenly round to his side, but in this play, as for the most part in real life, that does not occur. Our sympathy remains overpoweringly on the side of the victims. Sophocles is fond of repeating his effects, or rather of developing in one play an effect made more lightly in another. The heroic sister and the gentle sister appear as Electra and Chrysothemis, and more fully as Antigonê and Ismênê. The relation between Heracles and Deianira is perhaps a development of that between the harsh soldier Ajax and his gentle prisoner of war, Tecmessa. But one may ask why, if Sophocles wanted an unsympathetic hero, he should have chosen Heracles for the part. A certain type of critic is inclined to argue that if Heracles was recognized as "the best of men" and was actually, as we are informed from other sources, taken up to heaven in flames, it must follow that the pious Sophocles admired the qualities that most offend us and considered them to be part of the natural behaviour of a hero. Such critics tend towards a line of thought which over-emphasizes the alleged limitations of the Greek mind as compared with our own, a line which is sometimes of value in dealing with ancient politics and science but is badly misleading in the interpretation of great poetry. It flattens out all that is unusual into inoffensive commonplace, not realizing either the immense variety of Greek thought or the almost unlimited range of a great poet's creative imagination. If Sophocles and Shakespeare were not systematic psychologists like Aristotle and Professor Bain they had a creative insight into character which sometimes far outranged the professionals.

The subject is too large to be pursued here, but it is worth remembering that the great figures of Greek heroic tradition were never fixed by any definite historical record, but lived by floating in the minds of poets and their audiences. Hence they all change and vary, like Odysseus who is sometimes wise and heroic, and sometimes a mere villain. But none perhaps vary as much as Heracles. He is always "best of men" and "glorious conqueror" (*aristos andrôn* and *kallinîkos*), but the standards of goodness and glory change. He is originally "best" for the very simple reason that he beats all competitors, whether in trials of strength, of racing, of eating and drinking, and above all in the Games. He seems to have been originally a projection of the Kômos, or triumphant revel, of the victor. Indeed the Olympic victor actually received divine honours as having become Heracles or the local hero of victory. (See Cornford in *Themis*, chapter VII.) But in fifth-century Athens a different goodness, a different victory, seemed more worthy of the Best of Men. The simplest example is perhaps the famous allegory on the Choice of Heracles by Sophocles' contemporary Prodicus, in which the young man, facing temptation, decides firmly for Virtue as against Vice, for the steep upward path as against the easy. In Euripides' *Alcestis* Heracles is a jolly, hard-drinking reveller but with a hero's magnanimity and power in the background, when needed. In the same author's *Heracles* he is an heroic figure stricken down by the hate of a Goddess, but rising, with difficulty, to the almost intolerable ordeal of life afterwards. In later thought he becomes a saviour of mankind, or is allegorized into a saint and a philosopher. In this play, however, he is just the conqueror, the champion or prize-winner in battle and endurance. He shows none of the characteristic Greek virtues, no particular *Sophia* or Wisdom, no *Sophrosynê* or Temperance, no *Epieikeia* or generosity; no spark of mercy or gratitude. True he is a son of Zeus; that no doubt is the secret of his victoriousness, but it is no particular guarantee of moral virtue. Primitive gods are apt to be in Nietzsche's phrase "jenseits von Gut und Böse." In Sophocles as in Euripides the gods are often distinguished from human beings chiefly by their inhumanity, illustrated for example by the vindictive Athena of the *Ajax* or the malignant Apollo who is the source of all evils in the Oedipus. Among the more real and impersonal divinities we may think of the evil workings of Love described in two great lyrics of this play (497 ff. and 860 ff.), or remember the famous anecdote about Sophocles himself at the beginning of Plato's *Republic* where the poet rejoices to have escaped in his old age "from bondage to a raging madman." The piety of Sophocles insists mainly on the extreme danger of offending or disregarding the gods. Weak humanity must be always on its guard against powers so tremendous and so easily offended.

The chief liberty which Sophocles has taken with the traditional Heracles legend is that he entirely ignores his hero's deification. When Heracles is carried out to his funeral pyre there is not a word to suggest that he will be caught up to heaven in the mounting flames. It is a significant change. The idealized hero of legend or the philosopher's suffering champion of virtue might merit such an ending, but Sophocles cannot give it to the sort of Heracles he has chosen to depict. It is enough to pity his sufferings, to reflect on his victorious deeds of violence and cruelty, and to pronounce judgment that ultimately the author of all is not Heracles nor any human agent; all of it is Zeus—His will, His work, in a sense indeed Himself. (1264 to end.)

THE WIFE OF HERACLES

The date of the *Trachiniae* still remains uncertain. Probably most British scholars, from Jebb and Campbell to Mr. Kitto, have taken it as an example of Sophocles' later manner, but Professor Earp, in his very thorough and sensitive study of *The Style of Sophocles*, shows strong linguistic reasons for putting it early in the same group as the *Ajax* and *Antigone*. There is much Aeschylean magniloquence in the *Trachiniæ*, and that is normally a mark of the early style which Sophocles, by his own statement, grew out of. True, but how much must we allow for the archaic atmosphere of the play and the blood-and-thunder diction suitable to the "Ercles vein"? In Professor Earp's tables a very large proportion of the magniloquent words occur in Heracles' long speech (1046–1111) and in Hyllus' account of the burning robe (750–812) where they have some right to occur. And further, if the chief mark of the later style is its increased interest in *êthos* or character, the *Trachiniae* has that quality in a quite remarkable degree. Not only Heracles and his wife, but all the minor characters, such as Hyllus, Lichas, and the nameless Messenger, are real people, not merely instruments for declaiming speeches. So I still feel, on the question of date, that the verdict must be "Not proven."

CHARACTERS IN THE PLAY

HERACLÊS, the Hero, son of Zeus and the Theban Princess Alcmêna.

DEIANÎRA, daughter of Oineus, king of Pleuron and Calydon in the West of Greece, wife of Heracles.

HYLLUS, son of Heracles and Deianira.

LICHAS, herald to Heracles.

The NURSE of Deianira.

A MESSENGER.

An OLD SERVANT.

IOLÊ, daughter of Eurytus, king of Euboea, *persona muta*.

CHORUS of women from Trâchis in the hilly region of Eastern Greece, south of Thermopylae.

LEADER of the Chorus.

NOTE ON THE PRONUNCIATION OF NAMES

According to the current English convention, CH is pronounced like K; a circumflex accent ^ denotes that a vowel is long; thus Deianîra rhymes with Sapphira; Achelôüs with "below us," Alcmêna with "gleaner," while the *i* in Lichas, the *y* in Eurytus, the *o* in Iolê and the *a* in Omphalê are short. In this book I have only added the accents the first time that a name is used. The first syllable of Trâchis is like "ache"; and *a* in Oechalia, though short in Greek, may be pronounced as in Australia.

Zeus, the father of gods and men, is sometimes called by his Latin name "Jove," but Heracles is not given his Latin name, Hercules, because the associations of the Latin and the Greek are so different.

THE WIFE OF HERACLES

[In front of Deianira's house in Trachis: DEIANIRA
  standing centre, the NURSE *sitting in the background.]*

DEIANIRA.

There lives on earth an ancient word of light,
That no man's fortune can be judged aright
For good nor yet for evil, ere he die.
But mine: I need not wait for death, not I,
To know it an ill-starred and grievous thing.
Long since, in girlhood, dwelling with the King
My father, a great fear within me grew,
No maiden else in all Aetolia knew,
A fear of love; for to my wooing came
The daemon of a River, he whose name
Is Achelôüs. Changeful like a dream,
Three-fold he came; a towering bull, a gleam
Of serpent coils far-flung, a human form
Bull-fronted, and his shadowy beard a storm
Of rushing waters; in such guise did I
See love, and prayed in tears that I might die
Ere ever to those arms they brought me near.
Then, at the last, late, late, but passing dear
To me, there came the wondrous Son of Jove,
Alcmêna-born, and with that phantom strove
And me delivered. . . . How the fight was fought,
Ask me not ever, for I know it not.

If there be one who with unblinded eye
Looked on that battle, he may speak, not I.
I sate unseeing, trembling, lest for me
The gift of beauty mean but misery.
Howbeit, the God of Battles made that strife
End well . . . if well it be. Being chosen wife
To Heracles, still fear on fear doth press
Round me, amid his perils comfortless.
If night brings rest from pain, new pains and more
Wake in the night. The children that I bore
He scarce hath seen, like one who hath a plot
Of land o'er seas he knows not, visits not,
Save once perchance to reap and once to sow.
Such was the life that drove him to and fro
Unresting, labouring at a master's will.
Those toils, methinks, are done, yet graver still
My fears are. Ever since he dared to slay
Brave Iphitus, we are exiled, and I stay
In Trâchis in a stranger's house, while he
Is gone, none knoweth where, and leaveth me
More anguish than before. I know, I know,
He must have met some harm, to have vanished so,
All this long time. Twelve months and three have fled,
And still no herald. . . . Oh, for sure some dread
Mischance hath fallen. Was this the issue meant
By that dark tablet which, before he went,
He gave me and I kept? O God, I pray
'Twas not the symbol of an evil day.

                        [*The* NURSE *comes forward.*

NURSE.

My mistress, Deianira, long ago
I have seen what tears of thine, what signs of woe,
Have marked each going forth of Heracles.
But, if a thrall may dare, in times like these
To advise her masters, let me rise and speak.
Thou art rich in sons; should not a son go seek
His father, aye, and first the eldest go,
Hyllus, unless he careth not to know
Or good or evil of his father's fate?
But lo, how timely and with eager gait
Hither he comes! If in my word was aught
Well said, thou seest the man, thou knowst the thought.
                                        [*Enter* HYLLUS.

DEIANIRA.

My son, my child! From humble lips may fall
Wise words, methinks. This woman, being a thrall,
Hath spoke a word would well beseem the free.

HYLLUS.

How, mother? If not secret, tell it me.

DEIANIRA.

Doth it not touch thine honour not to know
Thy father's fortune, lost so long ago?

HYLLUS.

'Tis known—if one may trust the flying word.

17   B

DEIANIRA.

Where is he, then? What tiding hast thou heard?

HYLLUS.

'Tis said, this summer, month on month, he hath been
A house-thrall, servant to a Lydian Queen.

DEIANIRA.

He endured that? What will he stoop to next?

HYLLUS.

By that at least he is now no longer vexed.

DEIANIRA.

And now where is he hidden, alive or dead?

HYLLUS.

Against the isle of Eurytus 'tis said,
Some private war he is waging, or hath planned.

DEIANIRA.

(*startled*) My son! Thou know'st not. 'Tis about that
    land
He left with me a secret oracle.

HYLLUS.

I knew not that. What fate doth it foretell?

18

DEIANIRA.

An end of toil! Or death; or, after this,
A free life and long years of calm and bliss.
His life is trembling in the scale; go thou
And fight beside him. If he conquer now
We conquer with him; if he fails we fail.

HYLLUS.

Mother, I go. Had I but known this tale
Of dooms foretold, long since I had been there.
But, as things ran, I had but little care
Or fear. 'Twas ne'er the wont of Heracles
In battle to give cause for thoughts like these.
But now, having the knowledge, I will do
All things to find which of those ends be true.

DEIANIRA.

Go then, my son. To have done the right, though late
The knowledge came, must needs be fortunate.
[*Exeunt* HYLLUS *to his journey, the others to the House.*
Enter the CHORUS *of Trachinian Women.*

CHORUS.

[*Only the Sun, who sees all things, can tell where
Heracles is hidden. Deianira should trust in Zeus,
who will not forget his son.*]

Thou Child whom starry Night
Dies to bring forth and lays to rest in fire,

19

Sun, Sun, in heaven, give heed to our desire,
And show us where the Alcmena-born lies lost;
    Show us, thou fount of light!
Threads he some perilous channel of the deep,
Or far on one of the wide mainlands tossed
    Hath he found sleep?
Speak, thou whose eye rules all the realm of sight!

    For still with heart in pain
His Deianira, in hard battle won,
Like that sweet sorrowing bird that cries alone
At midnight, ceaseth not from longing vain
    Nor stills the lingering fear,
But on a bed of brooding, husbandless,
For her lost wanderer feedeth a great fear,
    Nursing her loneliness
With bodings that return again, again.

Waves ye have seen, before the unwearying wind,
Northward and southward towering and then gone;
So fall the Cretan seas in fury blind
On him, now whirling back, now lifting on.
But still there is some god who shepherdeth
His feet from that last edge whose name is Death.

I chide thee, tho' in love: 'tis no wise thing
To brood on thoughts that wear sweet hope away.
Never hath Zeus, the all-apportioning King,
Devised for mortal man a griefless day.

Sorrow and joy eternal wanderers are,
Winding they pass, as winds the northern star.

For nothing stays; not dancing Night,
Nor curse nor blessing; naught may last
For man. The moment flashes past
And on some other head hath cast
Its freight of downfall or delight.
But one thought cherish thou, my Queen,
'Mid all thy bodings lose it not;
Through all of time what man hath seen
The sons of Zeus by Zeus forgot?

DEIANIRA.

Dear maids, ye have heard, then, . . . else ye scarce were
      here . . .
My tidings; but the anguish of my fear
Ye know not yet. Long may it stay unknown!
For Youth in a sweet garden of its own
Groweth, all peaceful, where no burning heat
Of suns, nor rain nor storm wind vexeth it.
A girl's life is a fountain running o'er
With joys, until that moment when no more
Girl she is called, but woman, and must take
Her share of woman's cares, lying awake
In tears for child or husband. Then will she
Begin to learn the weight that lies on me.
Ye know of many perils that I have told
Ere now; but one more strange than those of old
Now presses. When for this last time my lord
Set forth, he left an ancient tablet, scored

With signs which, earlier, he had never cared
To explain, however dire the deeds he dared.
To conquer, not to die, was all his thought;
This time like a doomed man he spoke; he taught
All I must do without him: counselled me
Touching my part in his heredity
And how his sons their father's land should share.
He named a time; when he is gone one year
And three months, then shall he find peace at last.
Peace! Either Death or, once that day is past,
A free and griefless life for ever more!
Such was the doom, he said, the gods in store
Cherished, to crown the Toils of Heracles.
So spake of old the two Dove-Priestesses
Reading the whisper of Dôdôna's tree.
'Tis now that very time, and what must be
Shall be. O Friends, 'tis this that in the deep
Of night a-sudden starteth me from sleep
In terror, fearing to be left forlorn
Of the most glorious man of all men born.

LEADER.

Speak not of ill. One cometh even now,
With garlands of good tiding on his brow.

[Enter MESSENGER.

MESSENGER.

My mistress, Deianira, let me be
The first from all ill thoughts to set thee free.
He lives, he is victorious, and he brings
To Trâchis and her gods great offerings.

22

DEIANIRA.

What sayst thou, agèd man? What tale is this?

MESSENGER.

Right soon thy husband cometh, in the bliss
Of those proud arms that o'er all foes prevail.

DEIANIRA.

Who—citizen or stranger—tells this tale?

MESSENGER.

Lichas the herald in that grassy mead
Was speaking, where the herds in summer feed,
To a great concourse; straightway as I heard
I ran to be first bearer of the word,
And win some guerdon or good grace from thee.

DEIANIRA.

Bearing good news, why came he not to me?

MESSENGER.

It scarce was easy for him. In a ring
All Trâchis throngs around him, questioning;
Each hath his special care, and ere he know
That one thing, will not let the herald go.
'Tis their will, not his own, that in that place
Keeps him. Thou soon shalt see him face to face.

23

DEIANIRA.

O Zeus, who walkest Oitê's sacred mead,
At last, at last, thou hast brought us grace indeed.
Ho, women! Cry in joy, both ye who wait
Within my walls, and ye beyond the Gate,
In thanks for these great victories which rise,
Beyond all hope, like light before mine eyes.

CHORUS.

[Music and triumphal dance.]

LEADER.

O House, uplift thy voice!
    And jubilate thou Hearth!
A bridal song shall cry Rejoice,
    And shouts of men go forth,

MEN.

To thee, of the Quiver unfailing, Apollo, the Lord of
our choice.

MAIDENS.

And with them, O Artemis, maidens in joy shall their
    paean combine,
Thou torch-lit Ortygian huntress, to thee and the
    nymphs that are thine!

ALL.

A paean! A paean divine!

24

A Dancer.

I am borne on air, aloft, apart;
 Thy magic how can I repel,
O Bacchus, sovereign of my heart?
 I yield me to the ivy's spell;
It sweeps me in its whirling maze.
Praise be to thee, O Healer, praise!

All.

Euoi, Euoi! Paiân! Paiân!

Leader.

Belovèd bride, regard and see
That word of joy here visibly
 In shape before thy gaze.

Deianira.

Ha, maidens mine! Mine ever watchful eye
Fails not; see yonder a great company.

 [*Behind the rejoicing dancers enter* Lichas *the
  Herald, followed by a throng of Captive
  Women in extreme misery. Among them Iolê
  in particular is weeping.*

All hail, thou herald! Fortunate, though late,
Thy tidings . . .

     [*looking at the Captives*
   if these things be fortunate.

LICHAS.

Well-fortuned are we come, and crave some meed
Of welcome for our doings. He whose deed
Is fair must have fair words for his reward.

DEIANIRA.

Most sweet thy coming is; but of my lord
I first would learn. Comes he alive and quick?

LICHAS.

For sure I left him so; in no wise sick,
But full of life and health and strength of hand.

DEIANIRA.

Say on; was it in Greece or some strange land?

LICHAS.

There is a headland on Euboea's isle
Where to Kênaian Zeus he sought to pile
An altar and mark off due lines of land.

DEIANIRA.

Was that a vow? Or came there some command?

LICHAS.

A vow, when he set forth with sword and spear
To sack the city of these wenches here.

Deianira.

In pity's name, who are they? And to whom
Enslaved? Alas, 'tis so I read their doom.

Lichas.

From Eurytus' city; prizes he alone
Chose for the Temple's service or his own.

Deianira.

Was it against that city that he fought
So long, unheard of, lingering past all thought?

Lichas.

No, 'twas in Lydia, chiefly, so he told
The tale, he stayed perforce, a bondsman sold
In the slave market. . . . Mistress, take not ill
That name, when all the deed was by the will
Of Zeus. Aye, that whole year constrained was he,
He says, to serve barbarian Omphalê,
As bondsman. By which insult wounded sore
He bound himself with a great vow, and swore
One day to make the man whose folly gave
The start to that dire wrong, himself a slave,
With all his house. Nor was that menace vain.
Soon as his guilty hand was purged from stain,
A host he gathered and assailed the wall
Of Eurytus. That King, alone of all
Mankind, he held the author of his shame.
For once, when, being an old-time friend, he came

27

To Eurytus' hearth, his host did him much wrong
With mind malevolent and taunting tongue:
"Thou with the magic arrows, yet below
"My sons thou art in contests of the bow!"
Called him a servant, at a master's will
Chastised; then at a banquet, when his fill
He had drunken, flung him helpless from the door.
In wrath for that, one day when, searching for
Some horses lost, the King's son Iphitus
To Tiryns came and, standing hazardous
On the great tower, was scanning in all ease
The distant plain, a-sudden Heracles
Hurled him to death. For that sin Zeus, his sire,
But sire of all mankind, in righteous ire
Decreed that Heracles be sold a slave
O'erseas. No pardon for that blood he gave,
The only time thy lord had slain a foe
By treason. Vengeance in fair fight, I trow,
He blamed not; that were but just recompense;
For gods no more than men love insolence.
So all those men of pride and bitter breath
Are homeless now, save in the halls of death;
Their land enslaved; their women here we see,
No more in pomp and pleasure, sent to thee
As bondswomen. Such was thy husband's will,
Which I, his servant, faithfully fulfil.
Himself, when his thankofferings are done
To Zeus for that sacked city, as a son
Beseems, be sure he will rejoin thee here.
Of all my news, that most will please thine ear.

LEADER.

My Queen, thy hopes are won, one part full-pressed
And present, with clear promise of the rest.

DEIANIRA.

Surely I have full reason to be glad
Of this great fortune that my lord hath had.
I needs must match his joy with mine. I must . . .
Yet, after such great triumph, 'tis but just
To fear that some day later a reverse
May follow. Through my very soul doth pierce
An awful pity, seeing before mine eyes
These women, exiles under alien skies,
Wandering afar, homeless and fatherless;
Daughters of high-born houses, I should guess,
Who now must live the life of slavery.
O God of Battles, may I never see
'Gainst any child of mine thy fury thrust!
Not while I live be that, if be it must!
Ah me, the sight of these makes me afraid.
(*To Iolê*) Say, who art thou, O most unhappy maid?
Wedded or mateless? Surely, by thy face,
An innocent maiden and of noble race . . .
Lichas, who is this damsel? I would know
Her father and her mother . . . Why so slow
In answering? She methinks is worthiest
Of tears; she feels more, knows more, than the rest.

LICHAS.

How should I know? Why question me about
The girl? She comes of some good house no doubt.

DEIANIRA.

Princely, perhaps. What children had that king?

LICHAS.

I know no more. I did no questioning.

DEIANIRA.

Nor heard her name from any friend who knew?

LICHAS.

I talked not; I did what I had to do.

DEIANIRA.

Poor maiden, speak to me thyself. To be
Unknown and nameless makes life worse for thee.

LICHAS.

If any speech thou get from her, I vow
'Twill be a change from all we have seen ere now.
She never showed us any glimpse of what
She thought or felt. The whole time, speaking not,
Since once she left her city fallen and swept
By every wind, she hath only wept and wept.
'Tis not wise, but it makes one feel for her.

DEIANIRA.

Ah well, leave her in peace, and let her fare
At her own will beneath my roof. God knows
I would not make addition to the woes

That now she bears. Enough they are indeed!
But come, let us go in; so thou shalt speed
Thy journey, and I make ready what we need.

> [LICHAS *and the Captives go in. The* MESSENGER
> *holds back.*

MESSENGER.

One moment! Stay; and from the rest aloof
Learn who it is thou hast welcomed to thy roof.
There is a story here whereof thou hast heard
Nothing, but I can tell thee every word.

DEIANIRA.

What does this mean? Why wouldst thou stay my path?

MESSENGER.

Listen; if heretofore my story hath
Been worth thy hearing, 'tis no less so now.

DEIANIRA.

Wouldst have those men called back? Or speakest thou
Only to me and to my women here?

MESSENGER.

To thee and these. That herald can keep clear.

DEIANIRA.

Speak on and let us learn. He has gone his ways.

31

MESSENGER.

That herald . . . not a word of what he says
Is straight and honest. Either he lied to you
Here, or his earlier talk was all untrue.

DEIANIRA.

What mean'st thou? Open to me all thy thought.
Though plain thy speech I understand it not.

MESSENGER.

I heard him say—and many witnesses
Were there, to bear me out—that Heracles
Was wild to get this girl; he overthrew
For that Oechalia's mighty towers and slew
King Eurytus. 'Twas plain and simple love
Made him draw sword, not any gods above,
Nor Lydia nor the Lydian's slavish loom,
Nor Iphitus' carcase whirling to its doom.
'Twas love; which now this herald hides away
With fables that his former words gainsay.
No, first he pled to make her father thrust
This maid out privily to serve his lust;
That failed: then, on some lying plea, to exact
Vengeance he marched against her land and sacked
Her city; herself, thou seest, he has sent—
Home to this house—oh, not without intent,
Not as a mere slave; think it not! Desire
Has caught him and his flesh is all on fire . . .
I have thought it best to tell thee all I can,
My Queen, of what I heard from yonder man.

32

Many from Trâchis in that gathering came
Crowding about him; all have heard the same
And can bear witness . . . Surely, Queen, I rue
The pain I give thee, but I have told thee true.

DEIANIRA.

Woe's me! Where am I? Oh, what have I done?
I have taken to my hearth a poison, none
Deadlier, secret . . . . And she too in sore
Grief! Is she nameless as her keeper swore?

MESSENGER.

Not so; in race and name illustrious
She is, being daughter to King Eurytus.
Men call her Iolê—whom Lichas here
Knew nothing of, not having cared to hear!

LEADER.

Some knaves can be forgiven, but not he
Who adds foul treason to his knavery.

DEIANIRA.

Women, what shall I do? The things he hath said
Leave me all shaken and discomfited.

LEADER.

Go straight; question the man; methinks his lie
Will falter if thou force him to reply.

DEIANIRA.

Aye, well thou counsellest. I will seek him now.

LEADER.

While we await thee here? What biddest thou?

DEIANIRA.

Await me. . . . But self-summoned, see, before
I have spoke a word, he is standing at the door.

[*Enter* LICHAS.

LICHAS.

To Heracles hast thou some word to say,
Mistress? I now am starting on my way.

DEIANIRA.

So slow in coming and so swift to walk
Away, before we have had full time to talk!

LICHAS.

If thou hast further questions, I am here.

DEIANIRA.

Will thy replies be faithful and sincere?

LICHAS.

So help me Zeus!
As is my knowledge, so my speech shall be.

DEIANIRA.

Who is this woman thou hast brought to me?

LICHAS.

A young Euboean, but I know not how
Born or of whom.

MESSENGER.

[*coming forward*] Here, turn and face me thou!
Say, dost thou know to whom thou art speaking thus?

LICHAS.

Man, who art thou to stand there questioning us?

MESSENGER.

Answer me first, if thou canst understand.

LICHAS.

To Deianira, sovereign of this land,
King Oineus' daughter, spouse of Heracles,
My mistress—if this eye yet truly sees.

MESSENGER.

'Tis that, and simply that, I wish to know:
Thy mistress call'st thou her?

LICHAS.

Most rightly so.

35

MESSENGER.

And what due forfeit should'st thou rightly bear
If most disloyal thou art proved to her?

LICHAS.

Disloyal? How? What trap wilt thou devise?

MESSENGER.

Not I: 'tis all in thee the trickery lies.

LICHAS.

Farewell! I was a fool to give thee ear.

MESSENGER.

Not till on one brief point thou answer clear.

LICHAS.

Out with it, then. Thou hast no lack of tongue.

MESSENGER.

That battle-prize whom thou didst bring among
The captives here . . .

LICHAS.

I know. What is thy thought?

MESSENGER.

Didst thou not say—though now thou know'st her
  not—
That she was Iolê, child of Eurytus?

LICHAS.

Said it to whom? Who heard me speaking thus?

MESSENGER.

To a great concourse in the public square
Of Trâchis city. Many heard thee there.

LICHAS.

They say so?—Think you what some empty head
Fancies must needs be what was really said?

MESSENGER.

Fancy! Didst thou not tell us, in all ease,
Thou hadst brought her as a bride for Heracles?

LICHAS.

A bride for . . . My dear Mistress, graciously
Inform me, who may this strange person be?

MESSENGER.

One of that crowd to-day that heard thee tell
How 'twas for this girl's sake Oechalia fell.
That Lydian tale was naught. 'Twas his desire
For this girl wrapt her fatherland in fire.

37

LICHAS.

My mistress, bid this prater to be gone;
He is too brainsick to waste words upon.

DEIANIRA.

I charge thee in the name of Him on high
Who flames o'er Oitê's crest, seek not to lie
Nor shroud the truth. Thy story will be told
Not to a cowardly woman, but one old
In knowledge of man's heart, how it alway
Must change, and cares not in one joy to stay.
This god, Love—'tis a fool who dares to strike,
Front facing front, against him, boxer-like.
He throws the gods, they say; I know he threw
Me; and why not another woman too?
'Twere mad to blame my lord, if caught he were
In some such storm; aye, or to rail at her,
His partner in a state I know to be
No shame to them and sure no wrong to me.
All that is naught . . . If it was he who turned
Thy mind to lies, the lesson thou hast learned
Honours thee not. If 'twas thyself, thou'lt find
Cruel thou art in seeking to be kind.
Come, tell me the whole truth. To the free heart
The name of Liar hath a slavish smart,
Curse-like. And if thou thinkest to remain
Unquestioned and unproved, that hope is vain.
Too many have heard thee; some will surely tell . . .
Or art thou dumb from fear? It is not well

38

To fear so. Not to know the truth indeed
Would pain me; but to know, to know, what need
Pain me in that? Why, Heracles before
This time hath had his loves; Oh, countless; more
Than any man. Not one of whom hath heard
From my lips any blame or taunting word.
Nor shall this girl, not one; not though her whole
Being were sick with love. Nay, from my soul
I pity her. Her loveliness hath rent
Her life to shreds. Ill-starred and innocent,
She hath dragged to slavery and death her whole
People.—But all that down the wind may roll
Forgotten! Lichas, lie, if lie thou must,
To others, but to me, Oh, keep thy trust!

LEADER.

Hear her wise pleadings; thou shalt find them true
In after years, and win our blessings too.

LICHAS.

Belovèd Queen, human, as I see well,
Thou art, with human thoughts, and placable.
I tell thee, there is nothing I need hide.
True was this old man's tale that I denied.
A fatal passion for this damsel brake
On Heracles, and for her single sake
Blood-red Oechalia to destruction fell . . .
But, of him also the fair truth to tell,
In all this there was naught that he denied
At any time, naught that he bade me hide;

39

'Twas all myself, O Queen, fearing to wound
Thy heart with such a story, now am found
The offender, if thou tak'st it as offence.
But, now that the whole tale without pretence
Is known to thee, I beg thee for his sake,
And for thine own no less, endure to make
This woman welcome, and with steadfast will
Let these brave words thou hast spoken bind thee still;
Since he, the conqueror of all else, is laid
A prisoner in the dust before this maid.

DEIANIRA.

So speaketh my own heart . . . So will I do.
I would not add to all my pains the new
Affliction of a battle—vain, I know—
'Gainst the dark gods around us. Let us go
Indoors that I may think of messages
For him; a gift, too, in return for these
Thou hast brought us. Thou must not return again
Giftless, who camest with so great a train.

[*Exeunt into House.*

CHORUS.

[*The passion of Love, its power, its brutal
violence, its innocent victims.*]

Strong for all conquest is the Cyprian's power;
The fables of the gods I leave aside,
How fell the son of Cronos, and how fell
The great Earth-Shaker and the Lord of Hell;

But here, before our eyes, when came the hour
    To win this virgin bride,
What ravening arms reached out, what shapes uprose
To that brute rage of battle, amid blows
    And noise and blinding dust!

Here a bull phantom amid waters loud,
A crash of hoofs, horns towering through the cloud,
Sea-islèd Achelôüs swelled, and here
From mystic Thebes the Zeus-born raged with spear
And club and back-bent bow; so strove that pair
    Embattled, mad with lust,
Naught with them, naught above them, except Her,
    Cypris, in power alone.

All was a thud of fists, a deadly whirr
Of arrows, clash of wild-beast horn on horn
Grapples of writhing trunks, brows battle-torn
    And one o'ermastering groan;

While tender, beautiful, afar,
On the clear hillside, like a star,
Sitting she waits till it be known
Which brawler grasps her for his own.
As of a child that I had borne
I speak; that soft eye, battle-won,
Pitiful waiting, and then gone,
A young lamb suddenly alone,
    Motherless and forlorn!

          [*Enter* DEIANIRA *from the House.*

DEIANIRA.

Friends, while our guest withindoors doth prolong
His farewell parley with that captive throng,
I have stolen forth to find you, part in thought
To show you a device my hands have wrought,
And part to share with you the weight of fear
That fills me . . . I have taken to me here
This maiden . . . nay, no maiden she; this bride . . .
Like some dire secret cargo that men hide
In a ship's hold, a freight to wreck my peace.
Two women sleeping under the same fleece,
And held in the same arms: are such as these
To be our nights? And is it Heracles,
The true, the valiant, pays me this reward
For the long years I have spent in lonely guard
Over his house? . . . 'Gainst him, indeed, I ne'er
Could feel much anger. 'Tis the same old snare
Again hath caught him. But to live with this
New prize, to share with her his bed, his kiss . . .
What woman could endure it? And I see
Alway the flower of youth waning in me,
In her still lovelier opening; and man's eye
Clings to the fresh, they say, and hates the dry.
That is my fear; to find through the long years
The name and titles mine, the man all hers.
But anger, as I said, fits never well
With good sense in a wife. . . Friends, let me tell
A plan I have devised by which to find
Some path to peace, some medicine of the mind.

A charm, by beings of an older day,
Imagined, I have stored and hidden away,
In a bronze urn; a love-philtre which I,
Still a young girl, when he was like to die,
Gathered from Nessus, the great Centaur's, hide
Stained with his dying blood. Long years beside
Euênos' ford he used to stand, and there—
No oars, no sail—on his great back would bear
Travellers across the flood. I in that way
Was borne upon his shoulders on the day
When first my father sent me forth as bride
To Heracles. Out in mid stream he tried
In wanton arms to enfold me, and in fear
I shrieked, and in a moment past my ear
Heard Heracles' arrow singing. Fiercely through
That shaggy breast, piercing the lungs, it flew.
Then, faint to death, thus much the monster spake:
"Fair Child of ancient Oineus, thou shalt take
"One profit from my ferrying, if thou hast
"Care for my word, since thou shalt be the last
"That e'er I shall have borne across this flood.
"I charge thee, seek in the congealèd blood
"About my wound what drops of darkness, bred
"From Lerna's Hydra, tinged this arrow head,
"And thou shalt have a philtre so to bind
"The heart of Heracles that he shall find
"No woman fair, none worth his love, save thee."
When he was dead, that blood I tremblingly
Did gather up and in my chamber hide.
Which now remembering, I have subtly dyed

43

This tunic, duly pondering one by one
Each dying charge he gave. So now 'tis done.
Foul arts of witchcraft may I never know,
Please God, nor touch! May all who traffic so
Be accursèd! But a love charm, whose soft aid
May arm me against the beauty of this maid,
And wake in Heracles some tenderness
Of heart . . . well, there it stands prepared, unless
Ye judge there is some wickedness in what
I seek to do. If so, I do it not.

LEADER.

If thou hast ground for trusting in the spell
The elixir works, we think thou hast planned it well.

DEIANIRA.

I know not. A true promise in my thought
It seemed. No surer knowledge have I sought.

LEADER.

Knowledge must come from trial. Only so
Canst know indeed, not merely seem to know.

DEIANIRA.

That will I soon. Mark where the herald near
The doorway showeth. He will soon be here.
Keep well my secret; many a deed of name
Not seemly, if veiled in silence, brings no shame.

[Enter LICHAS *from the House.*

LICHAS.

Queen, I would crave thine orders, since my stay
Here hath been long and brooks no more delay.

DEIANIRA.

While thou wast with those damsels communing,
Lichas, my thoughts were on this very thing,
To send to my great husband by thy hand
This long robe, woven by me alone, and planned
For him alone. Bid him be sure that none
Before himself shall wear it: nor the sun
Touch it, nor any altar-fire nor flame
From any hearth, till he 'mid loud acclaim
Display it to the gods some day when high
Worship is held and bulls of offering die.
Long since I vowed, if I should see or learn
By trusty message of his safe return,
To clothe him in this robe, and in God's eyes
Exalt him, worker of a sacrifice
New, and in new far-shining garb arrayed.
In sign whereof a token I have laid
Here on the casket; he will quickly know
The impression of my ring—But go now, go!
And first remember, for a messenger
To do more than his office is to err.
Seek so to bear thee that from him and me
Alike due love and thanks may come to thee.

LICHAS.

A herald's duties I have long professed
And known, my Queen: I shall not fail thy hest
To hand our lord unopened, as it is,
This case, and add thy words as sureties.

DEIANIRA.

Then go thy way. All there may be to tell
Of our state here thou understandest well.

LICHAS.

I know and duly will report, O Queen.

DEIANIRA.

Speak of the foreign woman. Thou hast seen
She hath had from me good words and no annoy.

LICHAS.

I saw, and was struck dumb for very joy.

DEIANIRA.

What more is there to say? I only fear
Thy further speech. I would not have him hear
How my heart longs for him before I know
If he hath any care for me. Now go!

[Exeunt.

CHORUS.

[*An appeal to all the region of Thermopylae, the
Council Seat of Hellas, to rejoice in the return
of Heracles.*]

Ye watchers of Thermae's fountain,
 Where haven and rock divide,
By the vast Oetaean mountain
 And the midway Malian tide,
Ye men of the shore where dwelleth
 The maid of the Golden Bow
Where the spring of the Hero welleth,
 And the great Gates stand aglow
 When the Greeks to council go.

Soon, soon, shall ye hear the voices
 Of pipes not battle-mad
But sweet, as the lyre rejoices
 All earth when the Gods are glad;
For he of a mortal maiden
 And a high god deemed the son
Returneth in triumph, laden
 With spoils, his labour done
 And all his victories won.

Far over the sea belated
 He strayed, and never a word,
While twelve long months we waited,
 Was here of his tidings heard;

47

His listening bride heard only
> Her own sad heart complain;
Silent she pined and lonely;
> But War, now calmed again,
> Gives her escape from pain.

May he come! May he come, for pity!
> May his oarèd ship not rest
Till he come to his own dear city,
> From the shrine on the island crest
Where he makes to the gods his payment;
> May he come; and then all is well.
He will don the anointed raiment,
> And Love, by the centaur's spell,
> Through the whole of his being swell.

> [*Re-enter* DEIANIRA *from the House, troubled.*

DEIANIRA.

Women, I am afraid. I may have gone
Too rashly in this plan I have ventured on.

LEADER.

O royal Deianira, what hath passed?

DEIANIRA.

I know not, but I tremble, lest at last
There come from my great hopes great miseries.

LEADER.

It toucheth not thy gift to Heracles?

DEIANIRA.

Even so. Oh, never should man's heart be hot
To act in realms it understandeth not!

LEADER.

Tell, if it may be told, thy cause of fear.

DEIANIRA.

A thing hath come to pass . . . Oh, ye must hear;
A strange thing, of which no one could have thought.
A flock of soft white wool, wherewith I wrought
The anointing of that robe, hath vanished, died
Away to nothing, by no force outside
Consumed or handled. Self-devoured, away
It crumbled on a flat stone where it lay . . .
Friend, I would have thee know just what befell
And how. I needs must take more time to tell
My story. Not a word that, ere he died
In anguish from his arrow-piercèd side,
The monstrous Centaur spake did I forget.
Like laws engraved on bronze inviolate
I kept them. Fireless must the philtre stay,
In a shut casket, softened by no ray
Of sun, till I should take it out to spread
The unguent; so I had kept it. Now, I said,
The time was come. In my dark room alone
I spread it with a wool-tuft from our own
Sheepfold, and laid the whole robe folded tight
In a closed casket, hid from heat or light,

49   D

As ye all saw. But after, passing by
The doorway suddenly, there caught mine eye
A curious sight, scarce understandable.
It seems I had thrown down the shred of wool
I had used upon the robe, into a spot
Blazing with noonday sun. As it grew hot
It seemed to have shrivelled up; then in a while
Crumbled to powder. It was like a pile
Of wood dust made by a saw with fine thin teeth.
There lay it as it fell. And from beneath
The dry dust there were seething clots of foam,
Like the wine bubbles, frothing dark, that come
When Bacchic must is spilled. . . . Me miserable!
I know not how to think. Only too well
I see that I have done an awful deed.
What love was in that dying beast? What need
Had he to care for me, thro' whom he died?
None, none! 'Twas but by fooling me he tried
To work a treacherous vengeance on the foe
Whose arrow smote him. Why was I so slow
To see the truth, till all was no avail? . . .
No escape now! Unless all reasoning fail,
I am my husband's murderer. 'Tis decreed.
I know those arrows. They made Chîron bleed,
God though he was, in agony. They kill
Every wild beast they touch. The poison still
Was black and living in the blood that poured
From that deep wound. Must it not kill my lord?
I think so. Come what may, resolved am I,
If he must fall, I with him fall and die.

To live reviled and hated is no life
To one who has longed to be a blameless wife.

LEADER.

One needs must, in a life so tempest-tossed,
Fear; but, Oh, cling to hope till all be lost.

DEIANIRA.

Once the wrong road is taken, there can be
No turning back; nay, nor no remedy.

LEADER.

On sins unwilled, unwitting, there must light
A gentler wrath. Such pardon is thy right.

DEIANIRA.

There speaketh one who hath upon her thought
No guilt: not she through whom the wrong was
        wrought.

LEADER.

Enough. Refrain thee now and speak to none
Of this new dread; unless perchance thy son
Might help, here from his quest returned to thee.

> [*Enter* HYLLUS.

HYLLUS.

Mother, I would to God one fate of three
Were thine; or to be dead; or living still
To be no mother of mine; or that a will
New and less vile were in thy heart than now.

51

DEIANIRA.

My child, what have I done? Why shrinkest thou?

HYLLUS.

Thy husband, mine own father,—must it plain
Be spoken?—thou this day hast foully slain.

DEIANIRA.

Oh God, my son, what word has passed thy lips?

HYLLUS.

A word that ne'er shall fade into eclipse,
Since deeds once past can never be undone.

DEIANIRA.

What mean'st thou? Who accuseth me, my son?

HYLLUS.

I speak not from tales told. I saw him plain
Before me, dying, pierced by murderous pain.

DEIANIRA.

Didst find him, and stand by him at the last?

HYLLUS.

Thou wouldst that I should tell thee all that passed?
Back from the ravaged land of Eurytus,
With trophied arms and spoils victorious,

My father marched; but halted for a while
On a bold headland of Euboea's isle,
Kenaion called: there to All-Father Jove,
An altar he was marking, and a grove
Of shady trees. 'Twas there, my heart athirst
With joy and longing, I beheld him first.

    A vast blood-sacrifice he had in train,
With Lichas, his own man, returned again
From here, bringing the robe, thy gift of hate.
Obedient to thy word my father straight
Robed him. He then was slaughtering with strong hand,
As first fruits of his plunder of the land,
Twelve mighty bulls, but all in all that day
A hundred diverse victims he must slay.
There for a time, God help him! well content,
Proud of his robe and splendour, on he went
With the office, till a flame out of the blood
Of offering and the resin-scented wood
Blazed high: then all his body oozed with sweat,
And down his sides the soft silk clung, close-set
At every joint, as by some craftsman's art.
A piercing pain that rived his bones apart
Followed: it seemed through vein and flesh to make
A deep path, like the poison of a snake.
Sudden for Lichas then he called by name,
Lichas, who for thy doings hath no blame,
"By what foul plot had he this tunic brought?"
He made some helpless answer; he knew naught;
From thee alone, untouched by him, it came.
His master heard, and as a piercing flame

53

Tore at his lungs, caught Lichas by the foot,
Just where the ankle turns upon its root,
And hurled him flying 'gainst a sea-swept rock.
Out from the hair the white brain oozing broke,
And bone and blood fell scattered. A great cry
Of horror burst from all those standing by,
Seeing one man mad with anguish and one slain.
But none dared to come near him; for the pain
Now dragged him down, now made him leaping rise,
While that great voice was lifted up in cries
And groans of agony, till all around
The towering crags re-echoed, and the sound
Rang back from promontories mountain-high
In Locris and Euboea's rocky sky.
Till, spent at last, when the extreme of pain
Had mastered him, he cried again, again,
His curse upon the gifts thy father gave,
Thee and thy bed, abhorrèd as the grave,
Which all his pride of life so foully broke.
Then sudden thro' the shrouding altar-smoke,
A tortured eye uplifting, he descried
Me in the concourse weeping: "Son," he cried,
"Come close: thou shalt not from my torment fly,
"Not though it mean thou must beside me die.
"Lift me, and in some desert wilderness
"Set me, where none may see my last distress;
"Or, if that hurt thy pity, lift me clear
"At least of this vile land. I will not here
"Lie dead." We raised and softly in a boat
Laid him—it was not easy—and afloat

To this land scarce could bring him, still in pain
Fitfully groaning. Ye shall soon again
See him, or living or but lately cold.

    Mother, behold thy vile desire, behold
Thy deed: for which may Justice visible
Pursue thee, and the Erînys hot from Hell.
Thus, if God's Law gainsay me not, I pray,
Even I thy son: nor shall the Law gainsay;
Thyself hath wrecked all Law, thou who hast hurled
To death the man of all men in the world
Greatest, whose like shall never more be seen.

    [DEIANIRA *steals silently away into the House.*

LEADER.

Thou stealst away unanswering! Nay, O Queen,
Thy silence speaks to aid thine enemies.

HYLLUS.

Oh, let her go! Go! Vanish from mine eyes
Where'er the wind blows. "Mother"? Dare she claim,
Who hath no mother's heart, that sacred name?
Let her but go; and that same cup of joy
She gave my father, drink thereof and die! [*Exit* HYLLUS.

CHORUS.

[*The prophecy is fulfilled: Death is rest from
toil, and Heracles' rest can only mean death.
Deianira is innocent: the true cause of both his
death and his degradation is Love.*]

Behold, a-sudden here in the midst of us,
    Ye maidens, it hath lit——the ancient rede

God-spoken with foreknowledge marvellous;
Which lifted its great voice "So soon, so soon,
As fruiteth the twelfth harvest, moon by moon,
Then shall our Lord have rest, revealèd thus
    Zeus-born in very deed!"
True on the wind that word hath winged its flight;
For how shall he who no more sees the light
    Bear any toil or service? He is freed.

If still, amid that wound's blood-breathing spray,
    Guileful and unforgot, the Centaur's ire
Gnaws till the living flesh be eaten away
With poison old, born from the womb of death,
And ripened by the gleaming serpent's breath,
    How shall he see the sun beyond to-day?
      The Hydra's venom dire
Holds him encoiled, and 'mid the venom, lo,
Stab upon stab from that black-visaged foe:
    'Tis death, the lie, the poison, and the fire!

    Broke is the fount of tears.
A poison is poured out more dire than all
    That ever in past years
Hath wakened good men's pity or stayed the hate
Of envious foes against the heroic great:
    Well may we weep thy fall
When that dark spear, the front line battle's pride,
Drags from her hills one loath and flying bride.
Ah, plain the Cyprian standeth, secret-eyed,
    Silent, the cause of all!

56

Chorus.

[Separate members speaking.]

A.

How? Do I hear, or doth my troubled mind
Fancy that sound of weeping on the wind?
    Is it so? Hark!

B.

A sound there is; a voice only too clear
Of lamentation. Some new grief is here.
    And yonder, mark
That agèd woman, how with clouded brow
And pale she approaches. Ah, she calls us now.
                    [Enter the Nurse.

Nurse.

My children, great are the calamities
Sprung from our lady's gift to Heracles.

B.

Old Nurse, what new mischance hast thou to tell?

Nurse.

The silent Queen hath spoke her last farewell,
Gone her last journey with unmoving tread.

A.

Thou speakest not of death?

NURSE

My say is said.

A.

'Tis death!

NURSE.

Again I tell thee, she is dead!

A.

Unhappy! Lost! By what deed did she die?

NURSE.

A deed of cruel stress.

B.

What deed? Woman, reply!

NURSE.

Herself she found her way to nothingness.

B.

What passion, what sick thought,
On that keen evil edge cast her away?
One woman, and alone, how hath she wrought
Death after death this day?

NURSE.

Doth iron not bear a curse?

58

A.

The deed of wrath, didst see it, thou her Nurse?

NURSE.

I saw it. I stood near.

A.

What smote her? Oh, speak clear.

NURSE.

Her own hand, her own will ...

A.

Thy words are wild.

NURSE.

Nay, clear to all.

B.

(wildly) The bride hath borne a child!
The new bride borne a child!
A Fury and a Curse to wreck this Hall!

NURSE.

A curse incarnate! Ah, if ye had seen
That sight yet keener had your sorrow been.

LEADER.

A woman's hand could dare such deeds to do?

59

NURSE.

Dire deeds. But judge if I have spoken true.
    She went from here into the house alone
But there in the front court, seeing her son
At work upon a soft-thonged litter-bed
To meet his father on the road, she fled
In silence where she might be seen of none.
There, 'mid the altars kneeling, she made moan
Those altars should stay fireless evermore.
Then all the household gear she had used before,
When she was happy, she must touch again
With tears; so to and fro throughout the main
Castle she roamed, and if she saw some thrall
She had loved of old, she gazed, and shed withal
A farewell tear, revolving her own fate
And theirs, left masterless and desolate.
After a while she stayed; then suddenly
Toward his great marriage bower I saw her fly.
I followed and with screenèd eye could watch
All that she did. She turned aside to fetch
The princely robings of her hero's bed
And duly laid them; then, when all was spread,
On that high couch she cast her down, and lo,
The tears long checked burst in a burning flow:
"O home of love," she cried, "O bridal bower,
"Farewell for ever. Never from this hour
"Shall I, once your belovèd and your own,
"Lie here." Those words she uttered, those alone;
Then, with a sudden hand, tore from its hold
Above her breast the brooch of beaten gold,

And naked opened her left side and arm.
I with all speed dashed off to give the alarm
To Hyllus; but, too soon, before our aid
Could come, we saw her, that two-edgèd blade
Deep driven to reach her heart, to pierce her soul.
Oh, then her son in sobs outpoured his whole
Burden of grief; he knelt, pressed to his own
Those dying lips; then wildly flung him down
Beside her on the ground, with a great cry
That he himself hath slain her by that lie
Believed and spoke, and now he lingereth,
Unfathered and unmothered even to death.

    So is this great House fallen; Oh, fool and fond
Whoso the morrow morn or aught beyond
Counteth as sure. Shall he not learn at last
To-morrow is not till to-day be past?

                [*Exit* NURSE *into the House.*

CHORUS.

[*speaking severally*]

—Which sufferer should I first bewail?
—Which is more deeply pitiable?
—I ponder, but to no avail.

—The sorrow that we know is here,
—And that we know not hovereth near.
—'Tis one, to suffer and to fear.

61

—O Wind, would that some blast
　　Might sweep upon us with a wafting spell
　　To bear me far and fast
　　Away, away from here,
　　Lest, when God's awful Son I see
　　I die with fear—
　　Yea, at the mere sight, suddenly.
　　Soon, soon, in torment inescapable,
　　Greater than man, beyond speech marvellous,
　　He shall draw near to us!

> [*Enter slowly and in silence men carrying* HERACLES
> 　　*asleep on a bier. With them come* HYLLUS *and*
> 　　*the Old Servant.*

—Not soon, but now, close by,
　　Is that whereof, no nightingale more clear,
　　My heart gave warning cry:
　　Strange feet and alien faces drawing nigh!
　　Where take they him? In care for one so dear
　　Noiseless and slow they pass.
　　In utter silence he is borne; alas,
　　Think ye he slumbereth?
　　Or is this death?

> [*The bier is set down.*

HYLLUS.

　　Woe, Father! Woe for thee!
　　And I, what waiteth me
　　Now of new misery
　　To bear, what to redress?

62

OLD SERVANT.

Hush, O my son, let be,
Wake not to rage and pain
That sleeper merciless;
He lives, though overset.
Biting thy lips, refrain!

HYLLUS.

How sayst thou? Lives he yet?

OLD SERVANT.

Break not upon his rest,
Give not new life and eyes
To that fell haunting pest.

HYLLUS.

Nay, but on me there lies
Measureless misery.
Madness possesseth me!

          [He breaks down in tears.

HERACLES (*awakening*).

O Zeus, my father, where
Now, to what race of men,
Or what land am I borne,
By ceaseless torments torn?
Ah, me, despair!
It wakes, it gnaws again.

63

OLD SERVANT.

Were it not wise, o'er all
This wrong to weave a pall
Of silence, not to scare
Sleep from this sacred breast?
Oh, let him rest!

HYLLUS.

Nay, with such wrongs to face
How should I hold my peace?

HERACLES.

Thou great Kenaian altar-floor,
Gave I not blood enough to burn
On thy high places? What return
Is this? Oh, in God's name, what wouldst thou more?
Much mockery hast thou made of me.
Would I had seen thee not,
Known thee, nor felt thy hot
Madness unhealable!
For who by magic spell,
Who by the surgeon's knife,
Can save this stricken life . . .
Save Zeus? He! None but He!
The thought is but a dream of miracles
Seen afar off; what else? . . .
Oh, leave me to my rest, my last, last, rest!
Why touch and turn? What would ye now?
    Wouldst kill me, thou?
Yea, every sleeping pang thou wakenest.

64

It hath gripped me, it crawleth again. Ye men, is it
    Greeks ye be,
Ungrateful, for whose liberation I anguished in forest
    and sea,
And none in my sore affliction will succour me. Oh for
    a flame,
For a merciful sword, to smite this head from its body of
    shame!

OLD SERVANT.

Thou child of his loins, this task surpasseth all strength
    of mine.
Do thou lay hold, lay hold; for surely a power is thine
To save him greater than aught I know of.

HYLLUS.

                  I fold mine arm
About him, but neither within nor without can I find
    me a charm
To lift his life from its anguish. Such things are in God's
    decree.

HERACLES.

Where art thou, son? Is it thou?
Thus, ease me. Lift me now.
Is this then destiny?
It leaps now here, now there; it leaps to kill,
The accursed thing, savage, unseizable.
O Pallas, Pallas, again it racks me. O Son, give aid,
Have ruth for thy father! Strike, oh, strike with a
    blameless blade!

One stab from the bare neck downward, one stab would
     end this pain
Wherewith the godless woman, thy mother, hath
     maddened my brain.
O God let me see her yet struck down in agony,
The same, this very same, that now she hath wrought
     on me! . . .
O Hades, brother of Zeus, dear Death and dearly blest,
Send some swift-wingèd doom with rest from anguish,
     rest!

LEADER.

I tremble, friends, to hear those words and see
Such greatness so struck down in agony.

HERACLES.

Oh, many a fiery toil, yea, more than word
Can tell, these arms have sought, this heart endured,
But naught could ever the fierce Queen of Zeus
Devise, or mine old hater, Eurystheus,
Like this wherewith the crafty-smiling child
Of ancient Oineus hath my heart beguiled,
This devil's web that, cleaving to my side,
Hath ate my flesh within, hath drained the tide
That swelleth through my lungs, made its abode
Deep in the bone and drunk my leaping blood,
Till all my body is a wreck, alive
But death-bound, prisoned by this sightless gyve.
And this no fielded battle, no array
Of earth's gigantic brood, no beast at bay,

66

Naught, naught, in Greece nor Barbary nor the long
Leagues that I traversed cleansing earth from wrong,
Hath wrought; a woman, not a man, alone
And swordless, hath my greatness overthrown.
O Son, my own son, show thee mine in truth;
Hold thou no more in reverence or ruth
Thy mother's name: bring forth and with thine own
Two hands deliver into mine alone
The woman who gave thee birth. I fain would see
If more thou hast of grief for her or me,
When here in righteous doom before thine eyes,
Limb torn from limb, her mangled beauty dies.
Go forth, my son, and fear not. If there be
Ruth in thy heart, let it be ruth for me,
Whom all must pity . . . made to writhe and roar
Like a sick girl! And never man before
Hath seen me thus! Always without a sound
I followed where the road of hardness wound.
And now I am proved a woman! . . . Come to me,
My son. Stand close, and see what malady
Hath thus debased me. There. I lift the veil.
Look, all, and feast your eyes upon this frail
And tortured flesh. See what a depth of woe . . .
Ah, misery! Again a burning throe
Of torment stabs my side. No rest, no rest
Ever, from war with this devouring pest!
   O Lord of Darkness, take me!
   Smite me, O spear of Zeus!
Strike, O great king! Hurl, Father, through my head
Thy bolts! . . . Again this thing cries to be fed.

It flames. It rages . . . Hands, O hands I knew,
Shoulder and breast, O fore-arm ever true,
Are ye the same that in your strength of yore
Strangled that Nemean lion, from whose roar
The herdsmen fled as by the Alastor crossed;
Smote Lerna's Hydra, smote the Centaur host
Remote, outlaw, and monstrous, doubly strong,
Rider and steed, for every deed of wrong;
The boar on Erymanthus: and in Hell
The Hound Echidna-born, untamable,
Three-headed; and the Worm whose coils enfold
On the world's rim the fruit of guarded gold.
All these and other Labours have I won,
Countless; and none had victory o'er me, none.
And now, joints broken and flesh gnawed away,
To some blind curse I am flung a helpless prey,
I, first-born of the first of mothers, I,
Deemed Son of Zeus in heaven! Yet, though I lie
A thing of naught, here, moveless, yet give heed;
I swear the woman who hath done this deed
Beneath my dying hand shall meet her due.
Let her but come! Here she shall learn her true
Lesson and to the world of men confess
That, quick or dead, I have chastised wickedness.

LEADER.

Unhappy Hellas, what long grief I see,
Thy great protector lost, enfolding thee!

68

HYLLUS.

Father, thy silence gives me leave. Therefore
Give ear to what I say. I seek no more
Than justice . . . Prithee, listen in a mood
More calm than now, when anger fires thy blood.
Else thou shalt never learn how blind thy wrath,
Nor what poor hope thy cry for vengeance hath.

HERACLES.

Say what thou wilt and cease. I cannot spell
The sense of all this riddling parable.

HYLLUS.

My mother: of her state I have a word
To speak, how with no evil will she erred.

HERACLES.

Traitor! False Son! Ever to let me hear
That murderous mother's name! Hast thou no fear?

HYLLUS.

The time has come when all must needs be told.

HERACLES.

Thou hast some light upon her deeds of old?

HYLLUS.

On those of this day, as thyself wilt own.

HERACLES.

Speak; but remember still thou art my son.

HYLLUS.

My tale is this; she is dead, but newly slain.

HERACLES.

By whom? 'Tis strange . . . Must I be baulked again?

HYLLUS.

By her own hand, alone, with none beside.

HERACLES.

Curse her! By none but mine she should have died.

HYLLUS.

Even wrath like thine would melt if all were told.

HERACLES.

A strange beginning! Thy whole thought unfold.

HYLLUS.

She sought for a good end but lost her road.

HERACLES.

To kill thy father, villain! Was that good?

HYLLUS.

Seeing thy new bride, she found, as she believed,
A charm to win thee back, but was deceived.

HERACLES.

And where does Trâchis such wise charmers hold?

HYLLUS.

Nessus the Centaur counselled her of old
To use this charm thy lost love to regain.

HERACLES.

Nessus? God help me, then! (*A pause and complete
  change of manner*) All hope is vain.
I am undone, undone. For me the light
Shineth no more. Nay, now I know what plight
I am come to . . . Go, my son; thy brethren here
Summon, and her to Zeus so vainly dear,
Alcmêna. All of you before I go
Shall share the one last secret that I know.

HYLLUS.

Father, thy mother dwelleth here no more;
She lives in Tiryns, by the southward shore.
Some of thy sons she hath taken as her own
To cherish; others in the Thebans' town
Are gathered. We who are here and with thee still,
Father, in all things will obey thy will.

> [*At a sign from* HYLLUS *enter other sons of*
> HERACLES *with* IOLÊ; *they stand with the*
> *bearers.*

71

HERACLES.

Hear then my word. This day it is thy part,
Being called my son, to show what stuff thou art.
'Twas long foretold me by my Sire on high
That by no living hand His son should die;
Some dweller in the dark, long passed away
From earth, should slay me. And behold, this day
By that brute Centaur, living by the dead,
I am murdered, as the word of Zeus foresaid.
And later, too, strange oracles can I
Reveal, confirming that old prophecy.
Deep in the forest of that mountain folk,
The earth-sleeping Selloi, where my Father's oak
Speaketh with many tongues, its word of power
I noted, whispering that in such an hour
As now is here and living, my release
Should come and those hard Labours turn to peace.
I looked for days of leisure, and misread
A tale of death. No toil can touch the dead . . .
Since all these oracles toward one clear end
Are drawing, step thou forth and be my friend.
Pause not to think, lest thou provoke in me
Harsh words. Subdue thy stubborn will and be
My partner true. No other law is higher
Than this, in all things to obey thy sire.

HYLLUS.

Father, I tremble at this promise; still,
Where now we are come, I must obey thy will.

HERACLES.

Lay thy right hand in mine. That first of all.

HYLLUS.

What is thy purpose? Why so stern a call?

HERACLES.

Thy hand, quick! I will not be disobeyed.

HYLLUS.

I say no other. There; in thine 'tis laid.

HERACLES.

Now swear me by the head of Zeus, my sire . . .

HYLLUS.

To do what deed? Be plain with thy desire.

HERACLES.

To do what deed soe'er I bid thee do.

HYLLUS.

I swear. May Zeus to that oath hold me true.

HERACLES.

And if thou fail His curse be on thy head?

73

HYLLUS.

I shall not fail. Still, let that curse be said.

HERACLES.

Thou know'st Mount Oitê's crest, where Zeus doth
      dwell?

HYLLUS.

The place of sacrifice; I know it well.

HERACLES.

Thither upbear, I charge thee, in thine own
Arms, with such friends as thou canst count upon,
My body. There of oak deep-rooted hew
Branches abundant, pile them high, and strew
With faggots of the male wild olive tree.
Fling me upon that pyre. Then take to thee
A blazing pine-torch and set all aflame.
And let no tear come near me, no acclaim
Of sorrow. If thou art indeed my son,
Dry-eyed and silent do what must be done,
Else in the darkness I shall wait for thee
With wrath, thy curse to all eternity.

HYLLUS.

Father! What sayst thou? . . . Oh, thou hast done me
      wrong.

74

HERACLES.

I have said what thou shalt do. Else go. Belong
To others and be called my son no more.

HYLLUS.

For pity! 'Tis foul crime thou askest for,
To be thy murderer, reeking with thy blood!

HERACLES.

Not so; the final stauncher of this flood
Of pain, sole healer of my misery.

HYLLUS.

Can he who burns thy flesh thy healer be?

HERACLES.

If that affrights thee . . . wilt thou do the rest?

HYLLUS.

Thy body I will bear to Oitê's crest.

HERACLES.

And heap the oaken pyre as I command?

HYLLUS.

Save that I touch it not with mine own hand,
All else—thou shalt not blame me—I will do.

HERACLES.

So be it. It is enough. Yet add thereto,
After that service large, one slighter boon.

HYLLUS.

Be it or slight or large, it shall be done.

HERACLES.

Thou know'st, methinks, that child of Eurytus?

HYLLUS.

Is it of Iolê thou speakest thus?

HERACLES.

Even so. This charge I lay upon thy head.
If thou wilt show due memory of thy dead
Father, nor leave thine oath to him forgot,
Make her thy wife. Ha! Disobey me not!
No living man save thee shalt take as bride
The woman who once slumbered at my side.
My son, make thou that marriage bed thine own.
Consent. When grace in greater things is shown
It wrecketh all, in small things to rebel.

HYLLUS.

To strive with a sick man is pitiable,
But who could bear to see him so distraught?

HERACLES.

My wish, it seems, with thee counts less than naught.

HYLLUS.

'Tis she that caused my mother's death; 'tis she
Through whom all thine affliction came to thee;
What man not blinded by some evil-eyed
Demon, would choose that woman for his bride?
For me, my father, to share board and bed
With one I hate . . . Oh, liefer I were dead!

HERACLES.

Methinks he means to show me, as I die,
He cares not for me . . . Nay, God's curse shall lie
Upon thee if thou heed not my last call.

HYLLUS.

His madness soon will be made plain to all.

HERACLES.

Again wilt make my sleeping torture burn?

HYLLUS.

Ah me!
Doubt and bewilderment where'er I turn!

HERACLES.

Thou deignest not thy father's word to obey?

77

HYLLUS.

No, if a deed most impious bars the way.

HERACLES.

Not impious; 'tis the thing that most I need.

HYLLUS.

Thou givest me clear command to do this deed?

HERACLES.

The Gods be witness; 'tis my clear command.

HYLLUS.

The act is thine. I will no more withstand—
Hear me, ye Gods!—my father. It can be
No sin to sin in faithfulness to thee.

HERACLES.

Thou endest well. Now clothe thy promises
Swiftly in action, lest there rise from these
Torments again some stab, some rending fire,
Too soon, before you have laid me on the pyre.
Haste now, and lift me there. There waits my ease
From toil, and the last end of Heracles.

HYLLUS.

Enough. Thy will hath now an open way,
Father, and sore constrainèd we obey.

HERACLES.

O stubborn soul, set me a brake
On stony lips, steel-hard and true,
Now, ere the lurking pest may wake;
See there escape no sound from thee,
Since this last Labour thou must do,
Albeit constrained, is victory.

HYLLUS.

Lift him, ye thralls; and as ye see
The deeds here done, accord to me
Human forgiveness, and lay bare
The Gods' inhuman cruelty.
They get them sons; they bid us call
Them "Father," and then sit withal
To gaze on man's long agony.
What-shall-be none hath eyes to see,
But what-now-is doth but proclaim
The pitifulness of man, the shame
Of Gods; but most of all forlorn
Who bears the doom that thou hast borne!

CHORUS (to Iolê).

Maiden, arise! thou too must go;
   Forth must thy homeless path be trod.
Great deaths and strange 'twas thine to know,
Dire wrong and wondrous shapes of woe;
   And in them naught that is not God!

            [The procession moves off.

NOTES

NOTES

P. 19, l. 6 ff. Deianîra's father, Oineus, was king of Pleuron and Calydon in Aetolia near the mouth of the Achelôüs, the largest and most uncontrollable river in Greece. To get to Thebes or any part of central Greece she would have to cross the river Euênus, where the centaur Nessus (556 ff.) was in charge of the ford. Heracles was the son of Zeus and the Theban princess Alcmêna. He was doomed from birth to be servant to the King of Argos, Eurystheus.

P. 20, l. 27, "If well it be."] The doubt, though no doubt justifiable, is characteristic of the fearful and over-anxious Deianira.

P. 20, l. 38, Îphitus.] See 269 ff. P. 32.

P. 20, l. 40, "In a stranger's house."] that of Kêyx, king of Trachis, in the wild country south of Thessaly.

P. 22, l. 71, "He endured that?"] She feels keenly the slur on Heracles' honour.

P. 23, l. 86, "Mother, I go."] This is evidently Hyllus' first adventure. One must think of him as very young and impulsive. Hence his unhesitating fury against his mother (743–820), his passionate self-reproach afterwards (930–940) and his uncontrolled tears over his father's agony.

P. 25, l. 150, "Sons of Zeus by Zeus forgot."] Yet this son of Zeus will be either forgotten or betrayed. See end of play.

P. 25, l. 159 ff., "An ancient tablet."] Evidently Deianîra, true to the tradition of the heroic age, could not read. Phaedra could, and no doubt Mêdêa.

P. 26, l. 171 ff., Dôdôna.] The ancient priestesses at Dôdôna were called "Peleiades," Doves. They interpreted the sounds and movements of the sacred oaks, and no doubt wrote their interpretation out on tablets for those who consulted the oracle. (See 1167.)

P. 26, l. 177, "Garlands of good tiding."] Bearers of good tidings, especially if they came from a god (cf. *Oedipus*, 82 ff., where Creon comes from Delphi) wore wreaths visible from far off as a warning not to use ill-omened words or otherwise spoil the atmosphere.

P. 27, l. 192, "Why came he not to me?"] A sign among many of Deianîra's readiness to suspect that something is wrong. (Cf. 71, 246 ff.)

P. 29, l. 224, "Joy visibly in shape before thine eyes."] The dancers mean that their dance is "joy visible"; the dramatist, introducing at this moment the throng of weeping and dishevelled women, means: "Here is the thing over which you are rejoicing; look at it!" Hence the twofold effect on Deianîra.

P. 32, l. 270, Tiryns.] The ancient pre-Mycenaean castle in the Argive plain where Heracles lived.

P. 32, l. 287, "Thankofferings to Zeus."] Heracles is very assiduous and bountiful in his sacrifices to Zeus. Cf. the hecatomb of bulls and other beasts which he slaughters with his own hand (760 ff.). There is an atmosphere of slaughter about him.

P. 36, l. 367, "Not as a mere slave."] There was a great difference between having a "mere slave" as a concubine and bringing a princess, deeply loved, to the house to supersede the lawful wife. The first would have been venial misconduct, the second an outrage.

P. 37, l. 371, "Many from Trâchis—crowding about him."] It seems odd that Lichas, a well-trained professional herald, should have uttered this extremely confidential story to a great throng of people (cf. 423 ff.). Perhaps he told it confidentially to one or two and others heard it who were not intended to. There is a certain callousness about this messenger. He seems hardly to realize at first the effect his story will have on Deianîra.

P. 42, ll. 436–469. A wonderful and sincere revelation of Deianîra's character.

P. 44, ll. 496–530. The essence of this lyric is to depict love in man, or at least in this type of man, as a devouring rage, with the woman, at least this type of woman, as a victim, carried off "like a lamb from its mother."

P. 46, l. 541, "Is it Heracles, the true, the valiant?"] Her natural resentment against the great man bursts out occasionally in spite of her principles. Here it is corrected in the next line.

P. 47, l. 559, "Euênus ford."] See note on line 6. The Nessus incident varies slightly in the various Heracles traditions. If we are surprised that Deianîra should ever have believed that the dying centaur could wish to show special good-will to her (cf. 707) we must suppose that he had told her that he loved her. There was evidently a much longer conversation between them than is here repeated. (Cf. 580, 604 ff.)

P. 48, l. 581, "This tunic."] She here calls it a tunic. It was a peplos or long tunic reaching to the ground, such as was worn, Thucydides tells us, by the older generation of Athenians.

P. 51, l. 633 ff. Observe how Sophocles gets, somewhat artificially, a contrast by putting a joyful chorus just before the disaster. A very striking case is *Oedipus*, 1096 ff., where the chorus exults in Oedipus' unknown birth immediately before the fatal truth is revealed.

P. 55, l. 722, "Longed."] The Greek is rather "makes it her ambition." It has been a difficult task, but if she has failed in it she does not care to live.

P. 55, ll. 734 ff. Hyllus, always impulsive, breaks in with instant denunciation. His mother feels a shock at his shrinking from her and hopes against hope that all may not be lost; does she get some comfort at the thought that Hyllus "stood by him at the last"?

P. 58, l. 780, "Hurled him against a sea-swept rock."] One of the rocks in the gulf of Euboea, just south of Cape Kênaion, was supposed to have the outline of a human form. Hence a sailors' legend that it was a man flung there by Heracles, and the group was called "Lichades," much as stray rocks in Cornwall were supposed to have been thrown by the Devil, or, if there was a Pol-name in their neighbourhood, by St. Paul.

P. 58, l. 801, "Clear at last of this vile land."] It was infected with blood and death. Similarly in the *Trojan Women* the Greeks long to get away from Troy.

P. 60, l. 856, "That dark spear."] A difficult passage. I think the line of thought is: "Once his spear was always in the front line of battle; now all he can do is to ravish an unwilling and flying bride. Such is the work of the passion of love!"

P. 64, l. 911, "Masterless and desolate."] A mere guess at the meaning of a line generally despaired of by editors. "A great house left empty of servants" may imply, "servants without protectors." It might also be a reference to the "childless existences" of Alcmêna and of Deianîra's parents.

P. 66, ll. 956 ff., "God's awful son."] Note the terror inspired by the superhuman Son of Zeus, especially when distracted by pain, in which state he might do anything. Also notice in the following scenes the constant appeals to Zeus. Will the hero's divine father give him some supernatural help? See especially 1003, p. 68.

P. 70, ll. 1046 ff. This speech is rather finely translated by Cicero, *Tusculans* 2. 8. The translation is free, much compressed, and perhaps not free from mistakes. It is interesting that Cicero greatly softens the savage lines 1066 ff. ("Deliver into my hands," etc.), and omits the threat to tear Deianîra in pieces in the last lines of the speech.

P. 72, ll. 1091 ff., The Labours of Heracles.] The famous Labours are, first of all, services to the community which only the Best of Men can, or dares, perform; secondly they mostly seem originally to have been rustic achievements of a strong peasant working for a master. In the systematic mythologies they are Twelve, and are made heroic. Here we have only six mentioned; the Nemean Lion, the Hydra (or Watersnake) of the Lernaean Marsh, the Centaurs who disturbed the feast with Pholus, the Wild Boar of Erymanthus, Cerberus the three-headed watch-dog of Hades, and the Dragon which guarded the golden apples in the garden of the Hesperides. There is a list of eleven in Euripides' *Heracles*, including the Cerynaean Stag; the man-eating horses of Diomede, King of Thrace, the fight with Cycnus, son of Ares, and with the threefold monster Gêryon, the relief of Atlas in his toil of holding up the sky, and the capture of the Queen of the Amazons.

P. 72, ll. 1112, 1113, "Thy great protector lost."] These two lines of the chorus give one a slight shock. They have been taken to imply an admiration of all that the hero may do or say, including his proposal to tear his wife limb from limb, a conclusion which they will hardly bear. Obviously the Chorus are overwhelmed by the tremendous list of Heracles' achievements in destroying the enemies of man, and it would be going outside the function and manner of a Greek chorus if they qualified their admiration by adding a criticism.

THE WIFE OF HERACLES

P. 75, l. 1143, "Nessus? God help me then!"] Why does Heracles collapse so suddenly? I think that up to now he was in his heart expecting that Zeus would somehow save him, as he had done so often before. (119 ff.) The name of Nessus reveals to him that there is no hope; this is the fated and inevitable end. The shock makes him not only forget Deianîra—his natural self-centredness might explain that—but even forget that Alcmêna and most of his sons are not in Trâchis at all.

P. 76, l. 1166, "The earth-sleeping Selloi."] The Selloi were a tribe of very primitive habits who were in charge of the oracle in pre-Hellenic times.

P. 79, l. 1211, "If that affrights thee."] Curious that Heracles gives way on this one point, while in all else he is ruthless. As to Iolê, I think his motive is what he says. No stranger shall touch the woman who has belonged to him. The union of Hyllus and Iolê was in the legend; they were among the ancestors of the Spartan kings. It is significant that, of the two facts given in the tradition, the union of Iolê with Hyllus and the apotheosis of Heracles, Sophocles keeps the one that according to Greek feeling was discreditable to Heracles and omits that which tended to his glory.

P. 83, l. 1275, "Maiden arise."] It is not clear from the MSS. who speaks these last four lines nor to whom they are addressed.